DK SUPER History

UNDERGROUND RAILROAD

Learn all about the legendary secret network that helped liberate enslaved people in America during the 18th and 19th centuries

PRODUCED FOR DK BY
Editorial Just Content Limited
Design Studio Noel

Author Lisa Bolt Simmons

Senior Editor Ankita Awasthi Tröger
Editor Hattie Hansford
Senior Art Editor Gilda Pacitti
Graphic Story Illustrator Matt Garbutt
Managing Editor Carine Tracanelli
Managing Art Editor Sarah Corcoran
Pre-Production Coordinator Shanker Prasad
Pre-Production Designer Jaypal Chauhan
Production Controller Rebecca Parton
Publisher Sarah Forbes
Managing Director, Learning Hilary Fine

First American Edition, 2026
Published in the United States by DK Publishing,
a division of Penguin Random House LLC
1745 Broadway, 20th Floor, New York, NY 10019

Copyright © 2026 Dorling Kindersley Limited
26 27 28 29 30 10 9 8 7 6 5 4 3 2 1
001–350116–Feb/2026

All rights reserved.
Without limiting the rights under the copyright reserved above, no part of this publication may be reproduced, stored in or introduced into a retrieval system, or transmitted, in any form, or by any means (electronic, mechanical, photocopying, recording, or otherwise), without the prior written permission of the copyright owner.

No part of this publication may be used or reproduced in any manner for the purpose of training artificial intelligence technologies or systems. In accordance with Article 4(3) of the DSM Directive 2019/790, DK expressly reserves this work from the text and data mining exception.

Published in Great Britain by Dorling Kindersley Limited

HC ISBN: 979-8-2171-2562-3
PB ISBN: 979-8-2171-2561-6

DK books are available at special discounts when purchased in bulk for sales promotions, premiums, fund-raising, or educational use. For details, contact: DK Publishing Special Markets, 1745 Broadway, 20th Floor, New York, NY 10019
SpecialSales@dk.com

Printed and bound in China

www.dk.com

This book was made with Forest Stewardship Council™ certified paper – one small step in DK's commitment to a sustainable future.
Learn more at www.dk.com/uk/information/sustainability

Contents

Words in **bold** are explained in the glossary on page 44.

History in Perspective

For over four **decades**, more than 100,000 **enslaved** Black American individuals made their way to independence. They were known as **freedom seekers**. With the help of some brave people, they used a system of escape known as the Underground Railroad. This created a network of **activists** fighting for **abolition**.

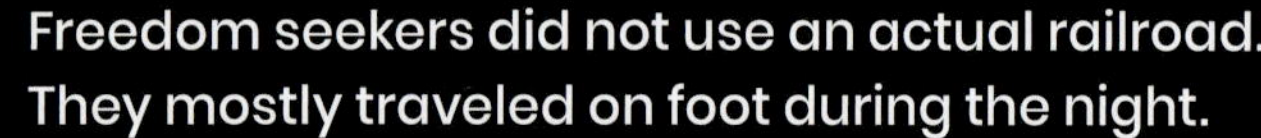

Freedom seekers did not use an actual railroad. They mostly traveled on foot during the night.

Where and when?

Many Black American people were enslaved in the southern United States. In these states, owning workers and treating them poorly was common. From 1820 to 1860, many enslaved Black American people ran away to find freedom on their own in the northern states. Over time, more white people began to see that **slavery** was wrong. They started to find ways to help enslaved individuals escape.

The Underground Railroad helped people fleeing slavery get from one point to another on their journey to freedom in the North. Not all white people believed in enslaving other human beings. Some families helped enslaved people. Many felt that slavery was a sin. Some people even believed that God would **condemn** those who enslaved others.

Think about it

We can learn about the Underground Railroad from newspapers, journals, diaries, and other written documents from the time. Most of these firsthand **sources** were written by white people. Why do you think that gives a limited view of what happened?

Who was involved?

People who helped freedom seekers went by different code words, such as "conductors," "stationmasters," or "engineers." These code words kept their identities secret. Free Black American people often helped enslaved people escape. Because of the dangers involved, most of the helpers will never be known. Many different elements contributed to the Underground Railroad cause, including **abolitionist** newspapers, speeches, books, and sometimes even violence.

Different perspectives

Different groups in society may have deeply contrasting experiences of events. Official records of the past often only present one side of the story. This means that they can't reflect the experiences of everyone affected. To understand what happened, it is important that we look at events from more than one point of view.

Key Events

WHAT HAPPENED WHEN

The fight against slavery grew stronger over the course of the 19th century. More and more white people joined the cause, both in secret and publicly. The Underground Railroad shows how Black American people led the way in seeking freedom and fighting for their rights. The movement was very important in helping many escape enslavement.

1826

OCTOBER

Levi Coffin settles in Newport, Indiana (now known as Fountain City). He and his family build a home that becomes a stop on three routes of the Underground Railroad.

1831

JANUARY 1

William Lloyd Garrison publishes the first issue of his newspaper, *The Liberator*. It openly criticizes slavery. Frederick Douglass, a formerly enslaved man, meets with Garrison to tell his story.

1833

DECEMBER

Garrison cofounds the American Anti-Slavery Society. The society encourages the **boycott** of cotton and other items produced by enslaved people. It also encourages **civil disobedience**.

1837

NOVEMBER 7

Elijah Lovejoy, an abolitionist printer, is murdered by a pro-slavery mob. This inspires John Brown to become an abolitionist.

1850

SEPTEMBER 18

The **Fugitive** Slave Act is passed by **Congress**. It gives people the right to capture runaways without **due process** or court proceedings. The act forbids anyone from helping fugitives or blocking **bounty hunters** from capturing them.

1860

From 1850 to 1860, the famous abolitionist Harriet Tubman travels back and forth 19 times from the South to the North. She leads more than 300 enslaved people to freedom.

1861

APRIL 12

The Confederate States Army fires upon Fort Sumter, South Carolina, marking the start of the Civil War. Starting in 1860, several southern states **secede** from the **Union** because they believe in the institution of slavery.

1865

APRIL 9

Confederate Army General Robert E Lee surrenders to Union Army General Ulysses S Grant. This is considered the beginning of the end of the Civil War. The last Confederate troops later surrender on November 6, putting an end to the fighting.

1865

DECEMBER

Garrison publishes his final issue of *The Liberator*. Georgia becomes the last state needed to **ratify** the Thirteenth **Amendment**. This makes slavery officially illegal in the United States. The Thirteenth Amendment forms part of the US **Constitution**.

Key People
WHO'S WHO

The Underground Railroad helped more than 100,000 enslaved Black American people find freedom in the North. Here are some of the key people in this story.

Abolitionists

William Lloyd Garrison
A strong **advocate** for abolition and nonviolence. He founded the weekly abolitionist newspaper *The Liberator*, which ran for more than 30 years.

Frederick Douglass
A formerly enslaved man who wrote a bestselling autobiography and published a newspaper called *The North Star*.

Harriet Tubman
Tubman was enslaved as a child but escaped to freedom in 1849. She helped other enslaved people find freedom.

Sojourner Truth
Truth was born free but was enslaved and forced into **hard labor**. She ran away to became one of the most famous abolitionists of the time.

John Brown
As a **Calvinist**, Brown believed all people should be treated equally. He also thought violence could be justified if it would end slavery.

Sojourner Truth

Conductors and stationmasters

Thomas Garrett
A stationmaster based for 40 years on the eastern route of the Underground Railroad.

Jermain Loguen
Loguen became famous for helping many enslaved Black American people escape to freedom in Syracuse, New York.

Levi and Catharine Coffin
A married **Quaker** couple. The Coffins hid freedom seekers in their house in what is now Fountain City, Indiana.

Leonard Grimes
A cab driver in Washington, DC. Grimes helped runaways escape by hiding them in his carriage. In 1839, Grimes was caught and sentenced to two years of hard labor.

William Whipper
A lumberyard owner. Whipper helped freedom seekers escape to Canada after the passage of the Fugitive Slave Act.

Leonard Grimes

Escaped and free

Tice Davids
Davids escaped enslavement in Kentucky in 1831 by swimming across the Ohio River. He was followed by his enslaver in a boat. Little is known of his fate.

Henry "Box" Brown
Enslaved in Virginia, Brown escaped by hiding in a box and shipping himself to the Philadelphia Anti-Slavery Society office.

William and Ellen Craft
A married couple who disguised themselves to travel to Philadelphia, Pennsylvania, by steamboat and train.

Solomon Northup
A free man from New York who was kidnapped and sold into slavery in 1841. He found freedom over 10 years later.

Ellen Craft

William Craft

Key Location
THE COFFIN FAMILY'S HOUSE

Secret Door

Basement

Levi and Catharine Coffin opposed slavery. They were determined to do what they could to help enslaved people who were trying to escape. In 1826, they moved to Fountain City, Indiana, which was then known as Newport. Their house was built in 1839 with special features to help freedom seekers. This two-story, eight-room house was home to the Coffins from 1839 to 1847. They lived there with their family. They also let freedom seekers traveling to Canada use it as a hiding place. It was such an important stopping point that it became known as the Grand Central Station of the Underground Railroad.

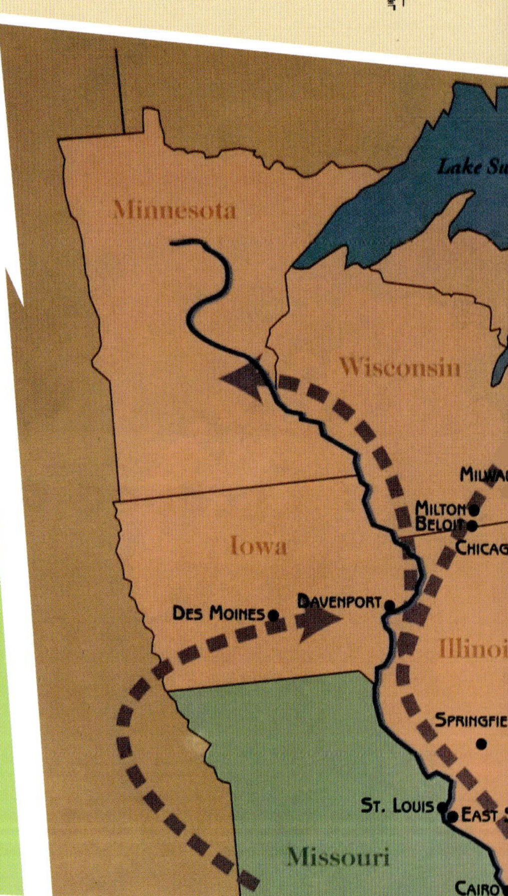

It is estimated that more than 1,000 freedom seekers used the house as a safe haven as they made their way to Canada.

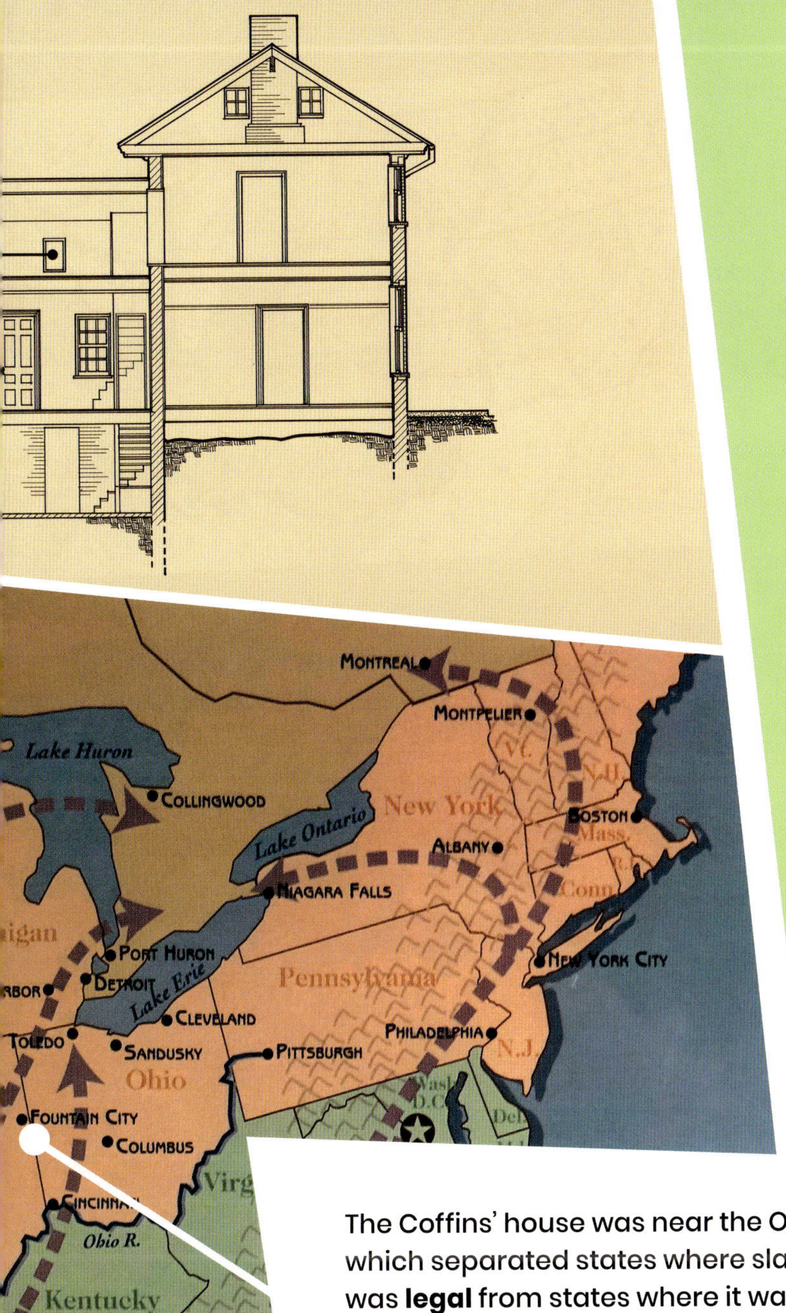

CLEVER DESIGN

The house was designed with plenty of places to hide, including a bedroom with a small door. The door was usually hidden from view by furniture and led to a secret space. The basement had a second kitchen and an indoor well.

The indoor well was fed by a fresh spring. It may have been used to supply freedom seekers with water without neighbors wondering why the Coffins were using so much water.

Today, the Coffin family's house is a museum that people can visit to learn more about the Underground Railroad.

The Coffins' house was near the Ohio River, which separated states where slavery was **legal** from states where it was not. The house was also close to the Indiana–Ohio border and allowed for different routes to Canada. For example, freedom seekers could travel through Ohio and Lake Erie, or through Michigan.

This map shows the main Underground Railroad routes as purple dashed arrows. These run from states shown in green that allowed slavery to those where it was illegal in orange. The state names and boundaries are given as they were during the period of the Underground Railroad.

A Nation Divided

When the constitution of the US was signed in 1787, it described freedom as a blessing. However, this freedom did not extend to the millions of enslaved people who were forced to work without pay, mostly in the South.

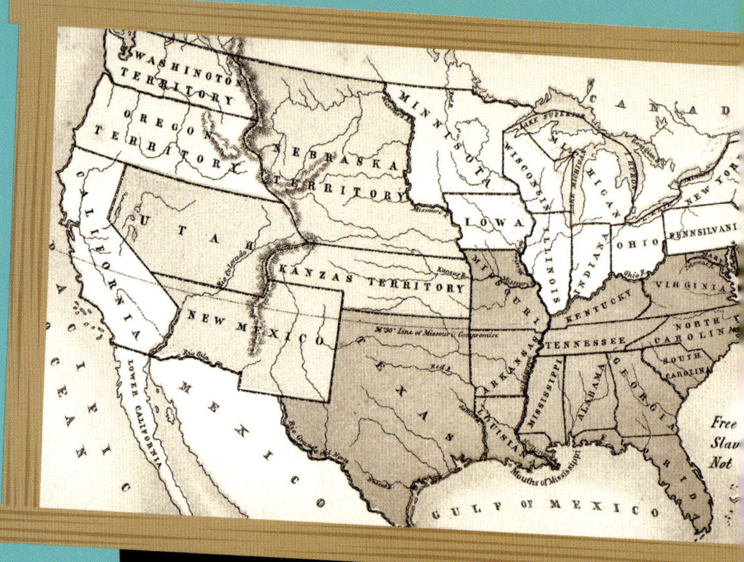

This map is from 1857, before the Civil War. The states shown with no shading were free. Those with darkest shading allowed enslavement. The other states had not yet entered the Union and were undecided on whether they would allow enslavement or be free states.

William Lloyd Garrison founded the New England Anti-Slavery Society and cofounded the American Anti-Slavery Society. Garrison believed in convincing people that slavery was wrong in nonviolent ways. He spoke and wrote about why everyone should be free.

MISSOURI COMPROMISE

By 1820 there was an equal number of states that did or did not allow slavery. Slavery was **outlawed** in Maine, so when it asked to join the Union people worried that free states would have more power. The US Congress allowed Missouri to join as a state where slavery was legal as a compromise. They thought it would keep things fair and balanced and stop arguments between the North and the South about slavery.

ANTI-SLAVERY SOCIETIES

The New England Anti-Slavery Society was formed in 1831. Within five years, it had local groups in Ohio, Massachusetts, and New York. In 1833, the American Anti-Slavery Society was founded. Just five years later, it had almost 250,000 members. Even though its members sometimes disagreed about politics and religion, they worked together to convince the public that slavery was wrong. They continued their work for many years, making more white people accept that slavery was wrong and cruel.

Frederick Douglass founded an anti-slavery newspaper called *The North Star* that was published from 1847 to 1851. He later edited two other newspapers.

BLACK ABOLITIONISTS

Although they had white **allies**, Black abolitionists and formerly enslaved people published their own newspapers. They also organized meetings. These groups played a huge role in the abolitionist movement.

Fascinating fact

Douglass was the most photographed American person of the 19th century. Over 160 portraits were taken of him. He believed photography was a powerful tool that could change views of Black American people.

Samuel Cornish was a **minister** and abolitionist. He believed slavery was wrong. Alongside John Brown Russwurm, Cornish published a newspaper called *Freedom's Journal*. In it, they hoped to tell the stories of Black American people free from the **bias** of white-owned newspapers.

Life Under Slavery

Enslaved individuals were considered to be property by their enslavers. On **plantations**, everyone had to work, even young children, elderly people, and those who were sick or hurt. Most enslaved people worked from dawn to dusk, six days a week. During the planting and harvesting seasons, they had to work 15 to 16 hours a day. At first, tobacco plantations were the most common. But during the 19th century, cotton became the most valuable **crop**.

On tobacco, cotton, and sugar plantations, enslaved people worked together in large groups. An **overseer** watched them.

HOUSEHOLD LABOR

Enslaved Black American people also worked in the big houses on the plantations. They cleaned, cooked, made beds, took care of the children, kept fires going, and carried out other household chores. Older or disabled enslaved people made clothes, spun cotton, and helped in the kitchen.

Enslaved Black American people were often sold at **auctions**. Since the marriages of enslaved people were not legally recognized, an enslaver could sell any family member at an auction and split up the family.

SLAVES!

ONG CREDIT SALE

OF

ANTATION HANDS

FROM ALABAMA, WITHOUT RESERVE.

Y N. VIGNIÉ, AUCTIONEER,

Passage, and corner of Conti street and

BRUTAL PUNISHMENT

Physical punishment was a fundamental part of the slavery system. Enslavers were often very cruel and used whipping as discipline. In extreme cases, chains and shackles were used for those who had tried to escape.

Think about it

The **mortality rate** was high for enslaved infants. About half died during their first year. The life expectancy of an enslaved person was only 21 years old. Why do you think this was?

INCREASED DEMAND

In 1793, an American engineer named Eli Whitney invented a machine known as the cotton gin. It removed seeds from the cotton fiber, making farming quicker and more **profitable**. As a result, more farmers wanted to grow cotton. This meant more enslaved people were wanted to work on the plantations.

REBELLIONS

Some enslaved Black American people fought for their freedom. Nat Turner led a group of other enslaved people to rebel against their enslavers. First, they killed Turner's enslaver and his family. By the time the rebellion had been stopped, they had killed 55 to 65 people.

Instead of reducing slavery, the cotton gin made it worse. Cotton plantation owners wanted more enslaved people to work in their fields.

Turner was caught two months after the rebellion ended. The event caused white politicians to pass stricter laws that further limited what enslaved people could do. Turner and many of his followers were later **executed**.

The Underground Railroad is Born

Many enslaved Black American people tried to escape their lives of **captivity**. Some wanted to visit family and friends for a short period, while others hoped to find freedom forever. But running away was very dangerous. This is why the secret system of the Underground Railroad was created to help them.

Images like this engraving of an enslaved Black American man running away were used on posters that offered rewards for the capture and return of freedom seekers.

People used whatever methods of travel they could to escape enslavement. This included wagons, horses, boats, and even trains.

ORIGIN OF THE NAME

No one knows for certain where the term "Underground Railroad" comes from. In 1831, Tice Davids fled from his enslaver's home and swam across the Ohio River while his enslaver chased after him in a boat. Once Davids reached the riverbank, he disappeared. It is claimed that his enslaver said that Davids "must have gone off on an underground road." No sources confirm if this is true, but people did start to use the phrase after this.

Isaac Hopper was a **liberal** Quaker and abolitionist. He helped the Underground Railroad in Philadelphia, Pennsylvania, and New York. By 1834, Hopper was well-known across the country, especially in New York, for housing freedom seekers.

QUAKERS

Quakers believed that slavery was evil. It was not allowed in their religion. Quakers who lived along the Underground Railroad did not turn freedom seekers away or return them to their enslavers.

MASON–DIXON LINE

Between 1763 and 1767, two English surveyors named Charles Mason and Jeremiah Dixon established the boundary between the major East Coast states of Pennsylvania and Maryland. This boundary was known as the Mason–Dixon Line. Before the Civil War, this line was the border between the South, where Black American people were enslaved, and the North, where they were free.

A survey marker stone from the 18th century. It shows the most southern point of the Mason–Dixon line.

SECRET NETWORK

It is not possible to trace the exact routes that runaways took, but we know most freedom seekers fled to the North. At first, they did so alone. But in time, many free Black American people in the North started to help. They formed groups to give food and shelter to freedom seekers, help them find work, and protect them from getting caught. These groups were known as **vigilance** committees.

Stealthy Stationmasters

Stationmasters were people who helped freedom seekers run away. They provided hiding places in their houses, or in buildings such as barns and warehouses. As more freedom seekers fled north, the Underground Railroad grew. More stationmasters were needed on the routes. These brave people played an important role in helping Black American people escape enslavement.

Thomas Garrett was a stationmaster on the eastern route of the Underground Railroad for 40 years. There was once a $10,000 bounty for his capture (about $378,000 in today's money).

Levi and Catharine Coffin's house in Indiana was positioned where three Underground Railroad routes met. They helped thousands of freedom seekers.

Presbyterian minister Reverend John Rankin and his wife Jean were stationmasters at their home in Ohio. They lived close to the Ohio River, which separated the free state of Kentucky from Ohio where slavery was still allowed.

Jermain Loguen was one of the most active stationmasters in the country.

NEW YORK STATIONMASTERS

The state of New York bordered free states and Canada, making it an important destination for many freedom seekers. In Syracuse, Jermain Loguen was a preacher and activist who is thought to have helped more than 1,500 Black American people find freedom.

In New York City, David Ruggles was the first Black bookstore owner in the United States. He sold abolitionist books, newspapers, and **pamphlets**, and also helped freedom seekers. His business was burned down twice, and he was attacked several times.

Stephen Myers helped hundreds of freedom seekers in Albany, New York. Stephen and his wife Harriet helped others for nearly 30 years and their house was the office of the Vigilance Committee of Albany.

This image is part of a cartoon by Edward Williams Clay called *The Disappointed Abolitionists*. The man portrayed in the middle is David Ruggles.

Stephen Myers was born enslaved but gained his freedom at the age of 18.

Courageous Conductors

As the struggle against slavery continued, courageous people became conductors on the Underground Railroad. Conductors helped move people from place to place. They risked their lives to help freedom seekers. Using local knowledge and skills, they guided freedom seekers along dangerous routes, often traveling at night. They provided transportation, shelter, and support.

Before becoming a minister, Leonard Grimes was an Underground Railroad conductor. He was a **hackman** in Washington, DC. It was the perfect cover to help runaways, as they would ride in his carriage on their way to freedom.

DANGEROUS WORK

Harriet Tubman was a famous Black American abolitionist born around 1820 in Maryland. She was enslaved as a child but escaped to freedom in 1849. Instead of staying safe, Tubman returned to the South many times to help others escape slavery on the Underground Railroad.

Think about it

What skills would have been important for conductors?

RISK-TAKER

John P Parker was sold and separated from his mother at the age of 8. He was forced to walk in chains from Virginia to Alabama in a line of enslaved people. He eventually bought his freedom and built a house in Ohio, where he worked and started a family. As a conductor, he took great risks, going to farms in Kentucky at night and bringing hundreds of freedom seekers to safety. Being a conductor was especially dangerous for Parker because bounty hunters knew who he was.

INTERNATIONAL CONDUCTOR

William Whipper was a successful business owner. He was the son of an enslaved Black woman and her white enslaver. Whipper first became a conductor in Pennsylvania. He helped hundreds of freedom seekers.

Whipper's family wanted him to move to Canada after people supporting slavery tried to burn down his business several times. Instead, he stayed in the United States, visiting his warehouse in Canada by railroad. The railroad cars contained secret compartments that freedom seekers hid in, allowing them to escape to Canada.

TRAGEDY TO TRIUMPH

Laura Smith Haviland was a Quaker who lost her husband, parents, sister, and youngest child to illness. Through her grief, she occupied herself with the abolitionist movement. Haviland helped freedom seekers move through Michigan, Indiana, and Ohio as they made their way to Canada. In this photograph she is holding some objects used to restrain enslaved people to raise awareness of the cruelty involved.

Journey to Freedom

Harriet Tubman
Enslaved woman and abolitionist

John Tubman
Harriet's husband

Ben Ross
One of Harriet's younger brothers

Henry Ross
Another of Harriet's younger brothers

William Still
A business owner and leading abolitionist

Born in 1822, Harriet Tubman was originally named Araminta Ross, or Minty. She grew up enslaved in Dorchester County, Maryland.

Araminta was often separated from her family as they all worked from a very young age.

Araminta learned from visiting sailors about a network helping enslaved people escape.

She married John Tubman, a free Black man, and changed her name to Harriet Tubman.

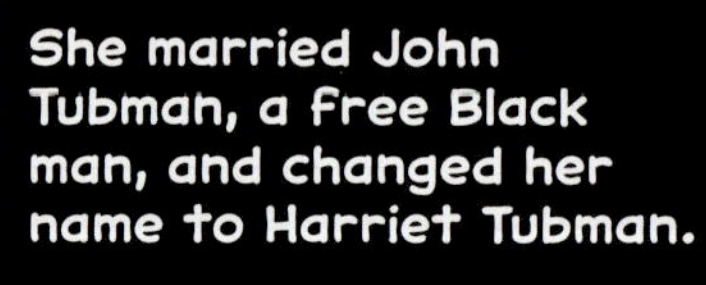

John did not share Harriet's dream.

When Harriet's enslaver Edward Brodess died in 1849, things got worse.
Brodess owed people a lot of money. They'll sell us down the river to pay his debts.
What do you mean, sell us down the river?
Down south, picking cotton. It's a lot worse than here. We may never see each other again.
What are we going to do?
Harriet planned the route, using what she knew of the paths across the marshy ground.
Harriet told her brothers of her plan to escape.
I know all the secret paths across the marshes. We can stay hidden.

On September 17, 1849, the escape began.
We need to get as far as possible before they discover we're missing.
We've decided not to go on.
We're going back. If we get caught, things will be worse.
I can't go back. One day soon, I'll come get you.
Harriet followed the North Star. She knew that she had to head north to find safety.
Harriet made contact with people from the Underground Railroad who helped her on her journey.
You are safe here. Don't travel during the day. There is a bounty for anyone who catches you.

Where am I?
You're in Pennsylvania. You're free, but be careful—you are never safe!
Harriet found work in hotels in Philadelphia. She planned to go back and rescue her family.
William Still was a stationmaster on the Underground Railroad.
Harriet met William in 1849 and offered to help others escape.
Mrs Tubman, you know that you'll be risking your life and your freedom as a conductor?
Mr Still, all my life I've wanted freedom for myself and my family. I will not give up.
Harriet Tubman made many trips to rescue enslaved people from Maryland, including her brothers and other family members.
I never ran my train off the track, and I never lost a passenger.

Working Undercover

The work of the Underground Railroad had to be done **undercover**. People caught helping freedom seekers suffered brutal physical punishments, imprisonment, and even execution.

Harriet Tubman

SECRET COMMUNICATION

Harriet Tubman used secret communication methods to send messages to freedom seekers. She sang certain songs, **mimicked** an owl, and mailed coded letters. Different songs, calls, or messages signaled it was time for runaways to keep moving or stay hidden.

CAREFUL PLANNING

Tubman risked her own life to help freedom seekers. She was very careful about how she traveled as she often went out at night. She carried a gun to protect herself and the people she was helping. Tubman knew she could be captured or even killed, but she kept going back to help more people escape.

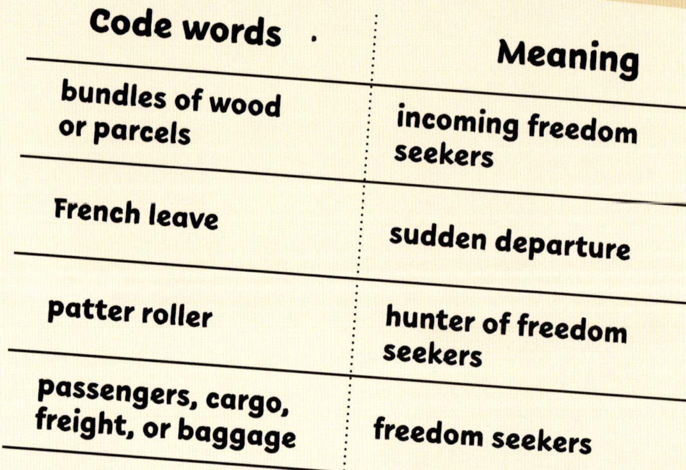

Code words	Meaning
bundles of wood or parcels	incoming freedom seekers
French leave	sudden departure
patter roller	hunter of freedom seekers
passengers, cargo, freight, or baggage	freedom seekers
tickets	freedom seekers on trains
freedom trails	routes
terminal, heaven, or promised land	northern free states and Canada

These are some of the code words Tubman used in her messages.

CODED QUILTS

Quilts have knots, shapes, and other symbols. Some historians believe these might have helped freedom seekers communicate their travel plans and send other coded messages.

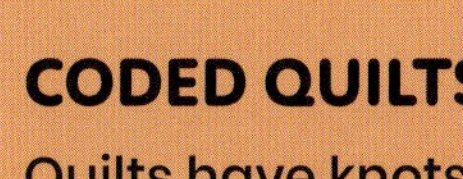

This quilt was made by Harriet Powers, a woman born enslaved in Georgia who later became free. Powers' quilts are now considered important pieces of American folk art.

Fascinating fact

Tubman used two songs to communicate with freedom seekers on the Underground Railroad. She would change the song speed so that runaways would know if it was safe to come out of hiding or if they should stay hidden.

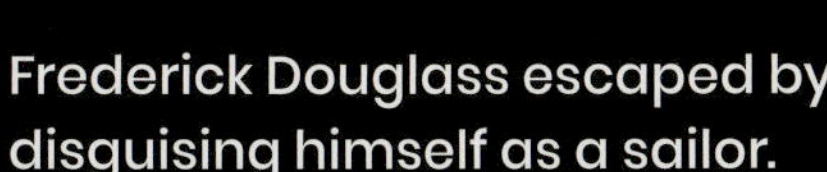

Frederick Douglass escaped by disguising himself as a sailor.

"FOREVER FREE"

As a child, Frederick Douglass learned the alphabet from Sophia Auld, one of his enslavers. Auld's husband would not allow her to continue teaching Douglass, because it was illegal. So Douglass taught himself to read and write. In his teens, Douglass was sent to work as a field hand under different enslavers. During this time, he taught other enslaved people to read and write. Douglass tried many times to escape to freedom before succeeding in 1838. Douglass famously wrote, "Once you learn to read, you will be forever free" (Douglass, 1845).

Famous Escapes

It took desperate acts for enslaved Black American people to reach freedom. Yet when they were finally free, sometimes they were still not safe. The threat of bounty hunters was never far away. Some formerly enslaved people fled to Canada, England, and other countries to keep their freedom.

HENRY "BOX" BROWN

Henry Brown was born enslaved in Virginia. At 5 ft 8 in (1.7 m), he was a tall man. To escape to freedom, he convinced Samuel A Smith, a white shoemaker, to ship him to Pennsylvania in a box that was 3 ft (1 m) long, 2 ft 6 in (0.8 m) deep, and 2 ft (0.6 m) wide. The box had tiny holes so that Brown could breathe, and he took a supply of water and biscuits with him. The box was marked "dry goods" and "this side up with care." But Brown spent hours upside down and almost died.

The box arrived at the Philadelphia Anti-Slavery Society office, where four people opened it. Brown stood up and shook their hands. He had spent 27 hours inside, but finally, he was free.

Ellen Craft in disguise, dressed as a white male enslaver.

HIDING IN PLAIN SIGHT

William and Ellen Craft were enslaved in Georgia by different enslavers. William convinced his wife, who had lighter skin, to dress up as his white male enslaver. Ellen could not write, so she pretended to have a broken arm. This way, no one would ask her to sign anything. William acted as her enslaved companion. On December 21, 1848, the Crafts set out on a four-day journey. They stayed at the best hotel in Charleston, South Carolina, and had breakfast with a steamboat captain. They rode first class on trains. When they arrived in Philadelphia, they were free.

William Craft

Ellen Craft

Two years after their escape, the Fugitive Slave Act of 1850 threatened the Crafts' freedom. They left for England, where they lived for 20 years.

THE LIBERTY LINE

In 1844, a Chicago newspaper called the *Western Citizen* published an advert for the Liberty Line. In reality, it was a reference to the Underground Railroad.

Written by Reverend John Cross, the advert invited those seeking better lives to use the route.

LIBERTY LINE.

NEW ARRANGEMENT---NIGHT AND DAY.

mproved and splendid Locomotives, Clarkson
dy, with their trains fitted up in the best style of
odation for passengers, will run their regular
ing the present season, between the borders of
archal Dominion and Libertyville, Upper Canada.
en and Ladies, who may wish to improve their
r circumstances, by a northern tour, are respect-
ited to give us their patronage.
TS FREE, *irrespective of color.*
ssary Clothing furnished gratuitously to such as
allen among thieves."

"Hide the outcasts—let the oppressed go
☞For seats apply at any of the tra
the conductor of the train.

J. CROSS,

N. B. For the special benefit of Pro-S
Officers, an extra heavy wagon for Texas, will be fu
nished, whenever it may be necessary, in which the
will be forwarded as dead freight, to the "Valley of Ra
cals," always at the risk of the owners.
☞Extra Overcoats provided for such of them
are afflicted with protracted *chilly-phobia.*

Think about it

Why do you think the *Western Citizen* editors printed the Liberty Line advert?

Risk of Capture

This image shows a freedom seeker being captured by a bounty hunter. The Fugitive Slave Act of 1850 encouraged ordinary citizens to help capture escaped enslaved people. People found helping a fugitive could be fined $500. That is about $20,000 in today's money.

When the US Constitution was written, Article Four laid out how the relationships between the states would work. It also included what is known as the Fugitive Slave **Clause**. This clause stated that all enslaved people who escaped to another state must be returned to their enslaver. Later, the Fugitive Slave Acts of 1793 and 1850 were passed to try and force all states to return runaways.

AN EVEN GREATER THREAT

The first federal Fugitive Slave Act was signed in 1793. This law guaranteed that enslavers could recover any runaways, as outlined in Article Four. But in 1850, a second Fugitive Slave Act went even further. It gave bounty hunters the right to search for suspected runaways and return them to their home state.

The act made it hard for escaped enslaved people to live safely in the northern states as it encouraged everyone to help catch freedom seekers. This meant that many people fleeing enslavement tried to reach Canada to secure their freedom. But even in Canada, life was not easy. Black people still faced unfair treatment. Many had trouble finding jobs and were often kept separate from white people.

KIDNAPPED

Solomon Northup was a free Black man living in New York. In 1841, he was kidnapped and sold into slavery. On the ship Orleans from Richmond, Virginia, to New Orleans, Louisiana, he was given the name Plat Hamilton. He worked on a cotton plantation before he was rescued in 1853. Northup published his autobiography, *Twelve Years a Slave*. This was later made into a movie.

do solemnly swear, to the best of our knowledge and bel
imported or brought into the United States from and after the first day of

This shipper's **manifest** is from the ship Orleans. It lists details about individuals on board the ship, such as name, age, sex, race, and height. On line 33, it lists Northup under the name of Plat Hamilton.

CAUTION!!

COLORED PEOPLE

OF BOSTON, ONE & ALL,

You are hereby respectfully CAUTIONED and advised, to avoid conversing with the

Watchmen and Police Officers of Boston,

For since the recent ORDER OF THE MAYOR & ALDERMEN, they are empowered to act as

KIDNAPPERS

AND

Slave Catchers,

And they have already been actually employed in KIDNAPPING, CATCHING, AND KEEPING SLAVES. Therefore, if you value your LIBERTY, and the *Welfare of the Fugitives* among you, *Shun* them in every possible manner, as so many *HOUNDS* on the track of the most unfortunate of your race.

Keep a Sharp Look Out for KIDNAPPERS, and have TOP EYE open.

This poster was published in Boston, Massachusetts, around 1850. It warns free Black American people about the risks of being kidnapped. Kidnappers would abduct Black American people and **smuggle** them into the South, where they could sell them into slavery.

After 12 years of enslavement, Northup was rescued and reunited with his family.

Fight for Abolition

The aim of the abolitionists was to secure freedom for all enslaved people. Abolitionists strongly believed that slavery was wrong and worked hard to end it. They organized rallies, wrote articles, and circulated **petitions** to raise awareness about the evils of slavery. They campaigned in the US and overseas.

Maria Weston Chapman founded the Boston Female Anti-Slavery Society in 1833. The group raised awareness and money to help fight slavery.

NARRATIVE

OF

SOJOURNER TRUTH,

A

NORTHERN SLAVE,

EMANCIPATED FROM BODILY SERVITUDE BY THE STATE OF NEW YORK, IN 1828.

WITH A PORTRAIT.

NEW YORK:

PUBLISHED FOR THE AUTHOR.

1853.

Although Truth never learned to read or write, she **dictated** her autobiography, delivered a famous speech about women's rights, and was invited to meet President Abraham Lincoln.

PREACHING THE TRUTH

Sojourner Truth (named Isabella Baumfree at birth) was born in New York in 1797. She was born enslaved, and was bought and sold four times before the age of 30. While enslaved, she was forced to do hard labor and suffered brutal punishment. After she had children, Truth ran away to an abolitionist family. They bought her freedom for $20. In 1828, she moved to New York City and worked for a local minister. She believed that preaching the truth was her calling. So, in 1843, she renamed herself Sojourner Truth.

ABOLITIONIST TRAVELER

Abby Kelley Foster spent more than 20 years traveling the country in the name of **social justice**. She was a national **delegate** in the Anti-Slavery Convention of American Women in 1837. In the 1850s, she worked for the American Anti-Slavery Society.

Foster believed that the inequalities experienced by Black American people and women were closely linked. She argued that both groups deserved the same rights and opportunities in society.

TO THE
RESCUE!!
TO THE CITIZENS OF COOPER:
We have just arrived from Kansas, having been ordered to return home by Col. Reid, for the purpose of raising a Company, of at least SIXTY men, to join him at Westport on the 13th inst., and in order to effect this object, we propose to hold a meeting at the Court House in the city of Boonville, on
MONDAY NEXT.
Let every man attend, and give us his counsel and advice; we want men who can be relied upon, men with strong arms and patriotic hearts, to stand by the gallant REID, and those who are now with him, upon the border of our State, to resist the aggressions of the lawless bands of abolitionists in Kansas.
J. W. DRAFFIN, H. H. BRAND,

People who supported slavery held their own meetings to share their beliefs. This advert from Arkansas calls for people to "resist the aggressions of the **lawless** abolitionists."

Fascinating fact

Gerrit Smith was a wealthy abolitionist and **philanthropist** from New York. He gave money to various individuals, groups, and social justice causes. It is estimated that he donated more than $8 million during his life. That's over $250 million in today's money.

Growing Desperate

Brown grew up in a very religious family who had strong abolitionist beliefs. He married twice and had 20 children.

Not all abolitionists believed in gradually and peacefully freeing enslaved people. Some wanted enslaved people and their allies to rise up and bring about an immediate end to slavery. One of these abolitionists was John Brown.

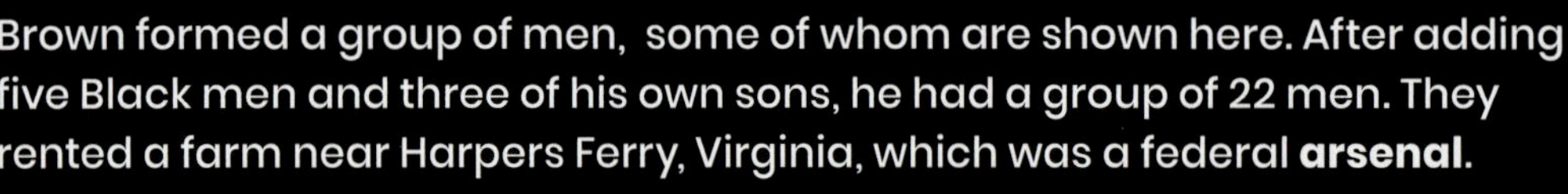

Brown formed a group of men, some of whom are shown here. After adding five Black men and three of his own sons, he had a group of 22 men. They rented a farm near Harpers Ferry, Virginia, which was a federal **arsenal**.

THE SECRET SIX

In 1858, Brown met with six important abolitionists. They were known as the "Secret Six." They planned to give Brown money to help fight slavery. They thought he was going to focus his efforts on Kansas. But Brown wanted to go to Virginia. This made the Secret Six nervous, although they were excited about what might happen.

HARPERS FERRY

Brown's aim was to start an uprising of enslaved people, using weapons from the arsenal. On October 16, 1859, Brown and his men took control of Harpers Ferry. They took hostages and killed five **civilians** in the process. News of their raid spread. On October 18, Colonel Robert E Lee, Lieutenant JEB Stuart, and a company of US Marines surrounded Brown and his men. They ordered Brown to surrender, but he refused. On the morning of October 19, the soldiers killed 10 of Brown's men, including two of his sons.

This engraving shows Brown being captured.

'REASON !

TRUE CHRISTIANS who believe in " Immortality
gh Jesus Christ alone," are requested to pray for

APT. JOHN BROWN,

now is under sentence of death, and is to be hung next
th for righteousness sake, and doing justly with his fel-
man, his country and his God.
y request of one who loves the Truth, and feels for the
that is to die a martyr to it. J.

ersworth, Nov. 4, 1859.

AFTERMATH

Brown was captured and accused of murder and **treason**. He was tried in court and convicted of all charges. He was executed on December 2, 1859.

Think about it

Despite his violent action, Brown was considered a hero by many people. Why do you think this was?

The Railroad's Impact

The Underground Railroad helped thousands of enslaved people escape to freedom. Although it did not end slavery, it played a critical role in challenging the institution, empowering enslaved individuals, and fueling the abolitionist movement. The movement was so powerful that it became a major reason why Confederate states sought to leave the Union.

THE CIVIL WAR

After President Lincoln's election, South Carolina seceded from the Union in December 1860. This was a sign of the unrest that would follow. From January to June 1861, 10 more southern states seceded. They wanted to keep the institution of slavery, and they were willing to fight for it. Civil war broke out between the North and the South in April 1861. The war centered on issues related to slavery and its expansion into new territories. The outbreak of the war ended the Underground Railroad's operations.

Abraham Lincoln did not want to see slavery expand in the United States, but he also did not call for abolition. This changed during the Civil War, when President Lincoln supported **emancipation** for all enslaved people.

Issued in Washington, DC on January 1, 1863, the Emancipation Proclamation declared that enslaved people in the states that had seceded were free. It meant that any persons escaping enslavement to states that were part of the Union were permanently free.

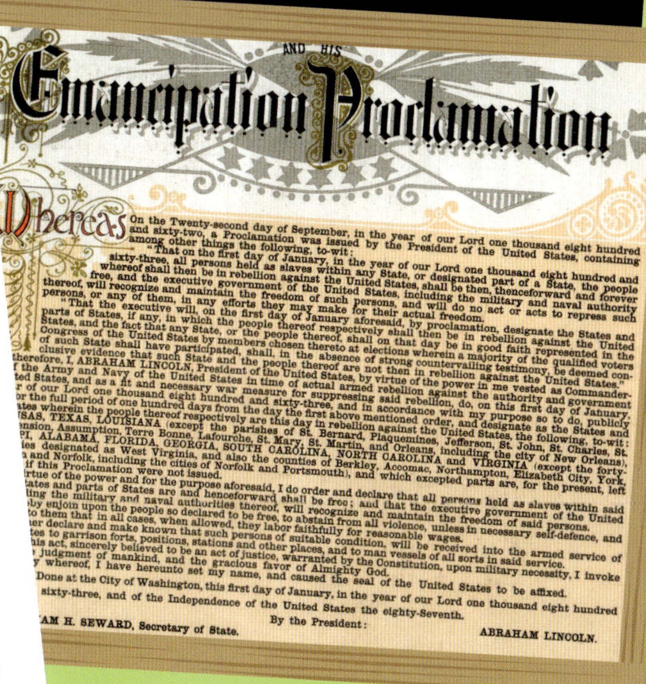

AND HIS

Emancipation Proclamation

Whereas On the Twenty-second day of September, in the year of our Lord one thousand eight hundred
and sixty-two, a Proclamation was issued by the President of the United States, containing
among other things the following, to-wit:
"That on the first day of January, in the year of our Lord one thousand eight hundred and
sixty-three, all persons held as slaves within any State, or designated part of a State, the people
whereof shall then be in rebellion against the United States, shall be then, thenceforward and forever
free, and the executive government of the United States, including the military and naval authority
thereof, will recognize and maintain the freedom of such persons, and will do no act or acts to repress such
persons, or any of them, in any efforts they may make for their actual freedom.
"That the executive will, on the first day of January aforesaid, by proclamation, designate the States and
parts of States, if any, in which the people thereof respectively shall then be in rebellion against the United
States, and the fact that any State, or the people thereof, shall on that day be in good faith represented in the
Congress of the United States by members chosen thereto at elections wherein a majority of the qualified voters
of such State shall have participated, shall, in the absence of strong countervailing testimony, be deemed con-
clusive evidence that such State and the people thereof are not then in rebellion against the United States."
therefore, I, ABRAHAM LINCOLN, President of the United States, by virtue of the power in me vested as Commander-
f the Army and Navy of the United States in time of actual armed rebellion against the authority and government
ted States, and as a fit and necessary war measure for suppressing said rebellion, do, on this first day of January,
r of our Lord one thousand eight hundred and sixty-three, and in accordance with my purpose so to do, publicly
or the full period of one hundred days from the day the first above mentioned order, and designate as the States and
ates wherein the people thereof respectively are this day in rebellion against the United States, the following, to-wit:
SAS, TEXAS, LOUISIANA (except the parishes of St. Bernard, Plaquemines, Jefferson, St. John, St. Charles, St.
nsion, Assumption, Terre Bonne, Lafourche, St. Mary, St. Martin, and Orleans, including the city of New Orleans),
PI, ALABAMA, FLORIDA, GEORGIA, SOUTH CAROLINA, NORTH CAROLINA and VIRGINIA (except the forty-
ies designated as West Virginia, and also the counties of Berkley, Accomac, Northampton, Elizabeth City, York,
a and Norfolk, including the cities of Norfolk and Portsmouth), and which excepted parts are, for the present, left
if this Proclamation were not issued.
rtue of the power and for the purpose aforesaid, I do order and declare that all persons held as slaves within said
tates and parts of States are and henceforward shall be free; and that the executive government of the United
ing the military and naval authorities thereof, will recognize and maintain the freedom of said persons.
by enjoin upon the people so declared to be free, to abstain from all violence, unless in necessary self-defence, and
to them that in all cases, when allowed, they labor faithfully for reasonable wages.
er declare and make known that such persons of suitable condition, will be received into the armed service of
tes to garrison forts, positions, stations and other places, and to man vessels of all sorts in said service.
his act, sincerely believed to be an act of justice, warranted by the Constitution, upon military necessity, I invoke
judgment of mankind, and the gracious favor of Almighty God.
y whereof, I have hereunto set my name, and caused the seal of the United States to be affixed.
Done at the City of Washington, this first day of January, in the year of our Lord one thousand eight hundred
sixty-three, and of the Independence of the United States the eighty-Seventh.
By the President:
AM H. SEWARD, Secretary of State.
ABRAHAM LINCOLN.

AFTER THE WAR

By the time the war ended and slavery was fully abolished in 1865, about 750,000 American people had been killed. In 1861, this was more than 2 percent of the population of the US. About 4 million enslaved Black American people were freed. The institution of slavery ended, although **segregation**, racism, and **discrimination** did not.

People gathered in Washington, DC to celebrate the abolition of slavery in 1865.

Lessons from History

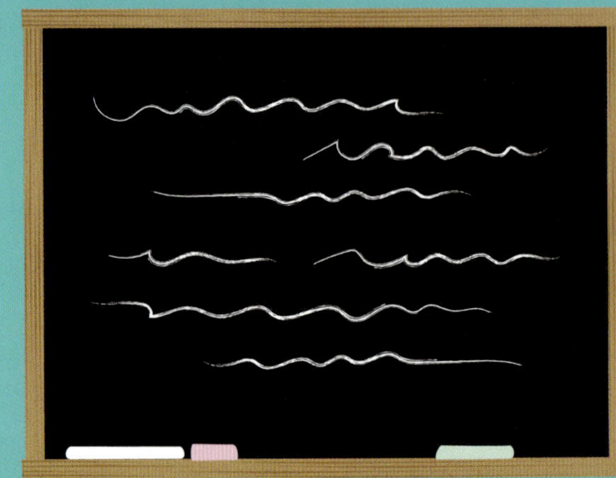

The Underground Railroad was a widespread network of individuals who worked together to help enslaved people find freedom. So why do we remember the Underground Railroad, and what can we learn from it?

UNTOLD STORIES

We know a lot about what happened on the Underground Railroad, largely from stories of those directly affected. Several formerly enslaved people wrote autobiographies, including Sojourner Truth and Frederick Douglass. These accounts allow us to learn about how they found freedom, and about their lives as enslaved people. But we do not know every story. Many people who escaped, or those who helped others, did not talk about it. Some could not read or write. We might never know about what they went through.

Think about it

Do you think we know the full story about the Underground Railroad? Do you think we ever will?

Harriet Tubman with her husband, stepdaughter, extended family, and some formerly enslaved people she helped to escape.

HARRIET'S LASTING LEGACY

Harriet Tubman will be remembered as an **integral** part of the Underground Railroad. She showed immense courage as she risked her life to escort people to freedom. During the Civil War, she was a nurse and spy for the Union Army. After the war, she continued to call for equality for Black American people and women.

FROM VILLAINS TO HEROES

At the time of the Underground Railroad, people who helped freedom seekers were breaking the law. The stationmasters, conductors, and others working undercover risked their lives to help freedom seekers escape. Now, many of these people are remembered as heroes. This gives us an example of how views can change. It also shows the power of coming together to fight for a cause. The Underground Railroad relied on the teamwork of many individuals.

The Tower Of Freedom in Canada was created by a sculptor called Ed Dwight. It is one of several monuments that help us remember those who were involved in the Underground Railroad, whether we know their stories or not.

A CONTINUED FIGHT

The end of slavery did not put a stop to racial inequality. Some people are still treated unfairly because of their skin color today. There is still work to do to make sure everyone is treated equally.

This photo is from a Black Lives Matter march in New York City in June 2020. At the march, protestors called for justice after a number of police officers killed Black American individuals, including George Floyd and Breonna Taylor.

Uncovering the Truth

A lot is known about the work of the Underground Railroad and the people it helped. This is because there are so many primary and secondary sources available. A primary source is a document or object created at the time of a historical event. A secondary source is a document or object created after the event, or by someone who was not directly involved in it. They can explain or interpret primary sources. They help in understanding an event.

Primary sources include

- official documents
- letters
- diaries
- paintings or drawings
- photographs
- sound recordings
- videos

Secondary sources include

- news articles
- books
- media documentaries
- encyclopedias

Photo of original source

DIFFERENT POINTS OF VIEW

Primary and secondary sources may tell different stories depending on the views of the people who created them. A person who agreed with slavery would have a different perspective than an abolitionist. It is important to question sources—doing this helps us to understand them and understand different perspectives better.

RECORD OF FUGITIVES

Although the exact routes of the Underground Railroad are not known, the stories of many freedom seekers are. This photo shows part of a page from Sydney Howard Gay's Record of Fugitives. Gay's office was an Underground Railroad stop and he kept records about the freedom seekers he helped. This is a primary source.

Original source text

April 3rd. Benjn. Moody. + James Cummens, belonged to Col. Jacob Hollingsworth, Hagerstown, Md. left in October.

Stopped all winter at Crosswicks, N.J. with Amos E. Middleton.

Forwarded to Syracuse, paying Benj.'s passage- 3.90

James C. left his mother, Mary Cummens. (Exs _ .25
+his sister Lucy at A. Middleton's.

Benjamin Moody and James Cummens are two of the freedom seekers who were recorded by Gay.

After their escape, they stayed with Amos E Middleton in Crosswicks, New Jersey.

Benjamin and James then went to Syracuse, with Benjamin's travel being paid for.

James left his mother and sister with Amos E Middleton. The notes include some abbreviations that are unclear to modern readers.

Look at the Record of Fugitives, then read the transcribed version of the text and answer the questions below.

Quick questions

- What is the name of the enslaver Benjamin and James escaped from?
- How many freedom seekers are recorded here in total?
- Who paid for Benjamin's travel?

Discussion questions

- Why was it helpful for the station masters to keep a record of people they helped?
- What sources would you look for if you wanted to better understand what it felt like to be a freedom seeker on an Underground Railroad route?

- Jacob Hollingsworth.
- Four: Benjamin Moody, James, Mary, and Lucy Cummens.
- The person writing the record (Sydney Howard Gay).

Vocabulary Builder
Secret Journeys

How would the Underground Railroad be reported today? Read this fictional article to see how a newspaper might have covered it at the time. Pay attention to key words that describe the work of the network and how people are responding to it.

THE PATHS TO FREEDOM

The southern states of the US are very angry. Their enslaved workers are finding ways to reach the North to gain their freedom. Plantation owners are blaming Black vigilance committees and white abolitionists for disrupting their lives. It is also believed that some citizens are helping to hide enslaved people in their homes.

Many people in the country have always opposed slavery. At first, Black activists started finding ways to help runaways find freedom. Then white abolitionists started helping the movement.

Abolitionist groups have been speaking out. More and more people are helping freedom seekers move north on secret routes.

In response to the controversy across the country, American people are leaning toward electing Abraham Lincoln as president. While he is not an abolitionist, Lincoln wants to keep slavery contained in the South. Some southern states are threatening to secede from the Union if he wins. American people must decide once and for all if they are for or against the enslavement of their fellow human beings.

Imagine you are writing a report about the work of the Underground Railroad. Then use the article on page 42 and the prompts and word bank below to write your own news story.

- **Why was the Underground Railroad needed?**
- **How did the network help freedom seekers?**
- **How did views about slavery differ across America?**

Describing slavery	injustice, bounty hunter, captivity, discrimination, fugitives, plantation, secrecy, segregation
Working for change	advocate, ally, backing, confrontation, encouragement, opposition, organization, resistance, solidarity
Actions taken	assist, boycott, conceal, disruption, guide, hide, protect, resist, shelter, support

Glossary

Abolition A movement working to end or stop something, for example, slavery.

Abolitionist Someone who worked to end slavery.

Activist Someone who works for or against an issue or cause.

Advocate Someone who works in support of an issue or cause.

Allies People who help and support other people who are part of a group that is treated badly or unfairly, even though they are not a member of this group.

Amendment A change in a law. In the United States, it is also an official change to the Constitution.

Arsenal A storage place for weapons.

Auction A sale of property to the person who bids the highest or offers the most money.

Bias An attitude that favors one view or position over another.

Bounty A reward offered for the capture of a fugitive.

Bounty hunter A person who tracked down fugitives for reward money.

Boycott The act of not buying or not using something from a company or country to show you disagree with its beliefs, policies, or methods. For example, if people do not like how a company treats its workers, they might stop buying its products to force it to change.

Calvinist A very strict group of religious followers who believe that people are predestined to go to heaven or hell.

Captivity Being kept in prison or otherwise not able to leave.

Civil disobedience A form of peaceful protest marked by the refusal to accept certain laws believed to be unjust.

Civilian A person who is not in the military.

Clause A separate part in a formal document.

Condemn To declare something is wrong or unfit.

Congress A body of government in the United States charged with discussing ideas and making decisions. It is made up of the Senate and the House of Representatives.

Constitution The written laws that govern the United States. The United States has separate constitutions for each state, in addition to the United States Constitution that applies to the entire country. Many countries have constitutions.

Crop A plant, such as a grain or vegetable, that is grown for harvest.

Decade A period of ten years.

Delegate A person who represents others at a meeting.

Dictated Speech that is written down.

Discrimination Unfair treatment due to prejudice.

Due process The right to fair treatment in the justice system.

Emancipation To free someone from control or the power of someone else.

Enslaved To be forced to work for someone else without the freedom to stop or leave.

Executed To be put to death as punishment for a crime.

Freedom seeker An enslaved person escaping to freedom.

Fugitive Someone who has run away.

Hackman A cab or carriage driver in the 1700s and 1800s.

Hard labor Very difficult manual work.

Integral To be an essential part of something.

Lawless To not follow any laws.

Legal To be permitted by law.

Liberal Used to describe the belief in individual rights and laws established for the good of the community.

Manifest A list of the cargo and people on a ship.

Mimicked To have copied someone or something.

Minister An official of the Christian church who often leads religious services.

Mortality rate The number of deaths in a specific population during a defined time period (such as a year).

Outlawed When something is made illegal.

Overseer A supervisor or superintendent.

Pamphlet A short, printed publication with no cover.

Petition A written request or demand for change, often including signatures of supporters.

Philanthropist A person who promotes goodwill and gives money to humanitarian causes.

Plantation An estate where profitable crops were grown.

Profitable Something that makes money.

Quaker A member of a religious group known for their values of peace, equality, and community.

Ratify To formally approve or sign into law.

Secede To withdraw from a larger unit.

Segregation To be kept separate due to gender, race, religion, or other factors.

Slavery A system in which people are owned by their enslavers and forced to work without pay.

Smuggle To export or import secretly and illegally.

Social justice The belief that all people in society deserve social, political, and economic equality.

Source A written document, artifact, or building that provides information relating to the past. Sources are also known as evidence.

Treason The act of betraying your own country by helping its enemies or by trying to harm it.

Undercover In secret, often while in disguise.

Union A name for the United States, and the name given to the northern states after the southern states had seceded.

Vigilance The state of being watchful in order to avoid danger.

Index

Acknowledgments

The publisher would like to thank the following for their kind permission to reproduce their photographs:

(Key: a-above; b-below/bottom; c-centre; f-far; l-left; r-right; t-top)

4-5 Alamy Stock Photo: Science History Images (t). **4 Alamy Stock Photo:** PAINTING (bl). **6 Alamy Stock Photo:** North Wind Picture Archives (c). **Getty Images:** FPG (cr); mikroman6 (br). **7 Alamy Stock Photo:** ClassicStock (br); Niday Picture Library (tr); IanDagnall Computing (bl). **8 Alamy Stock Photo:** GL Archive (b). **9 Alamy Stock Photo:** Heritage Image Partnership Ltd (tr); Reading Room 202 (cr). **Getty Images:** Heritage Images (br). **10-11 Alamy Stock Photo:** Randy Duchaine (b). **Library of Congress, Washington, D.C.:** Historic American Buildings Survery HABS_IND89_FOUCI1 (tc). **10 Alamy Stock Photo:** Stan Rohrer (bl). **11 Indiana State Museum and Historic Sites:** Courtesy of the Indiana State Museum and Historic Sites (br). **12 Alamy Stock Photo:** Alpha Historica (cl); Phil Cardamone (tc). **13 Alamy Stock Photo:** Yogi Black (br); IanDagnall Computing (t). **Bridgeman Images:** The New York Historical (bl). **14 Alamy Stock Photo:** GRANGER - Historical Picture Archive (b); history_docu_photo (tr). **15 Alamy Stock Photo:** Chronicle (br); Heritage Image Partnership Ltd (t); GRANGER - Historical Picture Archive (bc). **16 Alamy Stock Photo:** Photo 12 (t). **Getty Images:** clu (b). **17 Alamy Stock Photo:** Chronicle (tr). **Getty Images:** fotoguy22 (bl). **18 Alamy Stock Photo:** American portraiture (t); Chronicle (bl). **Ohio History Connection:** (br). **19 Alamy Stock Photo:** Historic Collection (t); Science History Images (bl); History and Art Collection (br). **20 Alamy Stock Photo:** Alpha Stock (t); Archive Pics (bl). **21 Alamy Stock Photo:** American portraiture (c); Design Pics Inc (t). **Getty Images:** Fotosearch (b). **26 Alamy Stock Photo:** RTRO (t). **27 Alamy Stock Photo:** Albu (t). **Getty Images:** Fotosearch (b). **28 Getty Images:** MPI (c). **29 Getty Images:** Chicago History Museum (b); Illustrated London News (t); Heritage Images (cr). **30 Alamy Stock Photo:** The Granger Collection. **31 Alamy Stock Photo:** AF Fotografie (br); Classic Image (cl). **The US National Archives and Records Administration:** (tr). **32 Alamy Stock Photo:** GRANGER - Historical Picture Archive (bc); piemags / DCM (t); incamerastock (bl). **33 Alamy Stock Photo:** Imago History Collection (t); The Picture Art Collection (bl). **34 Alamy Stock Photo:** IanDagnall Computing (t); World History Archive (b). **35 Alamy Stock Photo:** Historical Images Archive (t); Niday Picture Library (b). **36 Alamy Stock Photo:** Classic Image. **37 Alamy Stock Photo:** Everett Collection Inc (tl); World History Archive (cr); North Wind Picture Archives (b). **38 Alamy Stock Photo:** The Granger Collection. **39 Alamy Stock Photo:** Alpha Historica (t); NurPhoto SRL (c); Joel Villanueva (b). **40 Columbia Rare Book and Manuscript Library:** (bl). **43 Alamy Stock Photo:** North Wind Picture Archives.

Cover images: *Front:* **Alamy Stock Photo:** history_docu_photo br, PAINTING c, Pictorial Press Ltd t; **Photo Courtesy of Wofford Sculpture Studio, Cambridge, Maryland, © Wesley Wofford**; *Back:* **Alamy Stock Photo**: North Wind Picture Archives t, b; **Indiana State Museum and Historic Sites**: Courtesy of the Indiana State Museum and Historic Sites c.

Quote attributions:

Douglass, Frederick. 1845. *Narrative of the Life of Frederick Douglass, an American Slave*. Boston: Anti-Slavery Office.

All the books in the DK Super History series have been reviewed by authenticity readers to ensure the represented cultures and experiences are accurate.

This book uses language as appropriate to modern contexts. Historical terms that are no longer acceptable may be present in original source materials and images. These sources are included to present authentic insights into history.